Changes

S_____ays

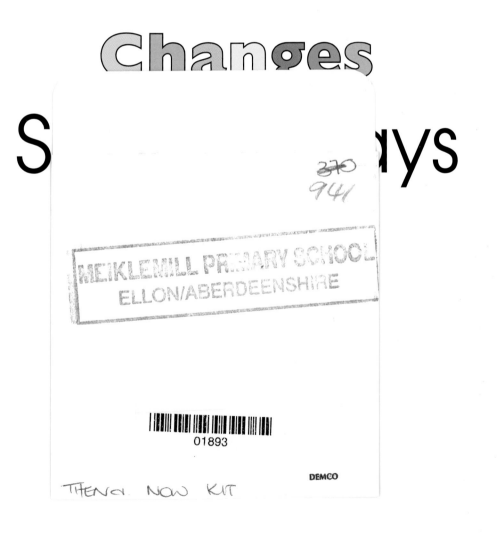

Project manager: Liz Gogerly
Designer: Peta Morey
Picture Research: Shelley Noronha at Glass Onion Pictures
Consultant: Norah Granger

Published in 2003 by Hodder Wayland, an imprint of
Hodder Children's Books

This paperback edition published in 2006

British Library Cataloguing in Publication Data
Gogerly, Liz
School days. - (Changes ; 6)
1. Schools - Great Britain - History - 19th century - Juvenile literature
2. Schools - Great Britain - History - 20th century - Juvenile literature
I.Title
371'.00941'09034

ISBN-10: 0 7502 3962 X
ISBN-13: 978 0 7502 3962 2

Printed and bound in China
by WKT Company Limited

Hodder Children's Books
A division of Hodder Headline Limited
338 Euston Road, London NW1 3BH

PICTURE ACKNOWLEDGEMENTS:
The publisher would like to thank the following for allowing their
pictures to be used in this publication:
Bridgeman Art Library /Private Collection 8 (top); Mary Evans 11 (top), 14
(top), 15 (bottom), 16 (top); Eyewire cover (main); Hodder Wayland Picture
Library 8 (bottom), 12 (bottom), 14 (bottom); Hulton Getty 4 (top), 5 (bottom),
7 (bottom), 13 (top), 18 (top), 19 (top and bottom); © Norfolk Museum
Services 12 (top); Photofusion 4 (bottom), 10 (bottom), 16 (bottom),
18 (bottom); Popperfoto cover (inset), (title page), 6 (top), 9 (top and
bottom), 10 (top), 13 (bottom), 17 (bottom); Topham Picturepoint 5 (top), 7
(top), 11 (bottom), 15 (top), 17 (top); Zul Mukhida 6 (bottom)

Contents

Getting Ready for School

Many children these days wear **school colours** or a uniform for school. Schools often have their own special **logo** or badge. In the past most children did not wear a uniform for school. They wore their ordinary clothes.

These **Victorian** girls have just arrived at school. The girls are doing exercises called a **drill** before they begin their lessons. Most of the girls are wearing white **pinafores**. The **pinafores** kept their dresses clean and were easier to wash.

These girls from the 1950s are walking to school. They probably went to a girls' **private school**. It was a **rule** that they had to wear school uniform. How can you tell they went to the same school?

This picture was taken in 1978. The teacher has just taken the **class register** and the children are lined up to go into class. The children at this school are not wearing a school uniform.

The School Building

There are many different kinds of school buildings. Some were built a long time ago and some are quite new. **Modern** schools often look different from some schools built a long time ago. Most of this **modern** school is on one level.

This photograph was taken in **Edwardian** times when this school was still quite new. It is built right next to the road. Boys and girls had **separate** entrances. Some of their lessons were **separate** too.

Schools built in the 1930s often had classrooms with doors that opened to the outside. This was to make sure there was lots of fresh air. Do you know when your school was built?

This school was built in 1900 but it was still being used in the 1960s. The building is very tall and there are **chimney pots** on the roof. How do you think the classrooms were heated when this school was new?

In the Classroom

In most classrooms children sit together around tables. The teacher has a desk but moves around helping everybody with their work. In **modern** classrooms there is usually a place where all the children can sit together with the teacher. Classrooms in the past looked very different.

In many **Victorian** schools all the classes fitted into one large room. Children usually sat in rows of desks. The teacher sat at the front of the class. This school is a special school for **deaf** children so some children are sitting around a table.

This picture was taken during the **Second World War**. Some children are sitting in rows. Other children are having a cookery lesson. There were often more than 40 children in a class.

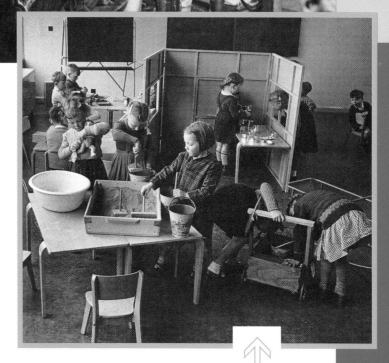

Schools built in the 1950s had more space for work and play. These children have a large play area. Does your classroom have an area to play like this?

Time for Lessons

During lessons children work in different ways. The whole class often works together with the teacher. Sometimes children work on their own, with a partner or in a group. The teacher is always there to help everyone.

In **Victorian** and **Edwardian** times the whole class had the same lesson at the same time. The teacher stayed at the front of the class. Children had to work by themselves. Everyone did the same work.

This is a classroom from the 1950s. The old desks have been pushed together so the children can work in groups. The teacher is reading to the class. See how the children have to share their books.

During this lesson in 1969 the teacher is reading to the children. They enjoy sitting together on the floor and talking about the story. Do you have any lessons like this in your class?

Helping Us to Learn

In the past school children did not have the colourful books or special **equipment** that you have in your class. They did not have televisions, **tape-recorders**, **overhead projectors** or computers. Today we have all these things and games and toys that help us with our lessons.

Many **Victorian** teachers had an **object box** filled with things like seeds, butterflies, pieces of material or string. Each week the teacher would select something different from the box for the children to talk about and draw.

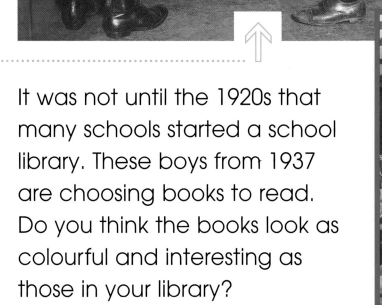

It was not until the 1920s that many schools started a school library. These boys from 1937 are choosing books to read. Do you think the books look as colourful and interesting as those in your library?

These children from 1952 were very lucky because they are watching a film. In those days there were not many televisions so this would have been a real treat.

Keeping Fit

These children are finding different ways of moving on the benches and mats. These days school children do many things to help keep them fit and **healthy**. They play games, dance to music and sometimes go swimming. In the past people thought it was important that children should be fit too.

In **Victorian** times children had to do exercises called a **drill**. The teacher would stand at the front and the children copied each movement they made. Boys and girls usually did these exercises **separately**. You can see the girls doing their **drill** on page 4.

These children from the 1930s are playing games to music to keep fit. Can you think of a game they might be playing?

By the 1960s many schools had **apparatus** in the hall for PE lessons. These children have changed into vests and shorts so that they can climb the ropes easily.

Taking a Break

After working hard at your lessons you need to take a break! In the past school was much **stricter** but children still had breaks. At lunchtime children could have a hot dinner or bring a packed lunch. In **Edwardian** times many schools did not provide dinners so children had to go home.

These **Edwardian** children are eating their school dinners. There is no school hall or dining room so they had to eat their lunch at their desks. Do you ever do this at your school?

From the 1940s to the 1970s most children had a school dinner. These children from about 1950 are served by the children wearing white **pinafores**. Only the older children could serve the food.

From the 1930s to the 1970s the **government** gave children free milk to drink at breaktime. These children from about 1960 also have a shop where they can buy sweets. Do you have a shop at your school?

Having Fun at School

There are many things to enjoy at school. Going on an outing, a visit to a **museum** or a **nature walk** can be very interesting. Special events in school are exciting. There were not so many interesting things for children at school a long time ago. But they did have some enjoyable times.

In **Edwardian** times school children usually went on a summer outing. Sometimes they even went to the seaside! For some children it was the only holiday they would have. Everybody wore their best clothes.

These children from the 1940s are making their own Christmas cards. They are making prints using **lino** and ink. What kind of cards do you make in class?

Putting on a school play can be a lot of fun. It is a chance to sing, dance and act in front of your school and parents. These children from the 1950s are **rehearsing** for a **Nativity Play**.

Notes for Parents and Teachers

Changes and the National Curriculum

The books in this series have been chosen so that children can learn more about the way of life of people in the past. Titles such as *A Bite to Eat, Beside the Sea, Dressing Up, Home Sweet Home, School Days* and *Toys and Games* present children with subjects they already know about from their own experiences of life. As such these books may be enjoyed at home or in school, as they satisfy a number of requirements for the Programme of Study for history at Key Stage 1.

These books combine categories from 'Knowledge, skills and understanding' and 'Breadth of study' as required by the National Curriculum. In each spread, the photographs are presented in chronological order. The first photograph is a modern picture that the child should recognize. The following pictures are all historical. Where possible, a wide variety of pictures, including paintings, posters, artefacts and advertisements have been selected. In this way children can see the different ways in which the past is represented. A lively selection of pictures also helps to develop the children's skills of observation. In turn, this will encourage them to ask questions and discuss their own ideas.

The text is informative and raises questions for the children to talk about in class or at home. It is supported by further information about the historical photographs (see right). Once the children are familiar with the photographs you could ask them to guess when the pictures were taken – if it isn't mentioned in the text. By looking at clues such as clothes, hairstyles, style of buildings and vehicles they might be able to make reasonable guesses. There are further questions to ask your child or class on the right.

About the Photos

Getting Ready for School
Pages 4–5

Pupils of Townsend Road School during a drill in 1905
Questions to ask:
- How old do you think the girls are in this picture?
- Do you think this was a good school to go to?

No information about this photograph
Questions to ask:
- Can you describe the girls' uniforms?
- Do people who help you cross the road look like this today?

Children in the playground in 1978
Questions to ask:
- How old do you think the school in this picture is?
- What do you think the classrooms inside might be like?

The School Building
Pages 6–7

Staff and pupils outside the Beckett Road School in Doncaster
Questions to ask:
- From what was this school building made?
- Do you think it was dangerous that the school was near the road?

Children taking physical exercise at Hartfield Crescent Elementary School, Birmingham *circa* **1930s**
Questions to ask:
- Do you think this school looks light and spacious?
- How many windows and doors can you see?

The Michael Faraday School in 1968
Question to ask:
- Can you tell from the photograph when this school was built?

In the Classroom
Pages 8–9

The Deaf and Dumb Institution, Derby *circa* 19th century
Question to ask:
- Do you think it must have been difficult to work in classrooms like these?

Pannal Council School, Harrogate, during the Second World War
Questions to ask:
- What do you think the children sitting down are learning about?
- Do the pupils in the kitchen look older than those sitting down?

Birley School in Derbyshire in 1953
Questions to ask:
- Do you think the children in this class are enjoying themselves?
- Do you think this classroom is well equipped?

Time for Lessons
Pages 10–11

A school in Doncaster, date unknown
Questions to ask:
- Do you think sitting in rows with the teacher at the front was a good way to learn?
- Why do you think the boy is with the teacher at the front of the class?

A teacher reading to the class at Hallfield School, Paddington, 1950s.
Question to ask:
- How similar is this classroom to yours?

The head teacher reading to her pupils at Beckford Infant's School, West Hampstead, London in 1969
Question to ask:
- Do you think the teacher is reading an interesting story?

Helping Us to Learn
Pages 12–13

A Victorian teacher's object box
Questions to ask:
- Can you name any other things in this box besides those mentioned on page 12?
- Would you enjoy describing and drawing the objects in this box?

A group of schoolboys selecting books at Rotherhithe's LCC School library, *circa* 1937
Question to ask:
- Is this library similar to the library at your school?

Education films being shown to 5-year-olds in a Surrey School in 1952
Questions to ask:
- Can you see what the children are watching on the screen?
- Can you describe how the classroom is set out?

Keeping Fit
Pages 14–15

Boys doing exercises in the grounds of their school, *circa* 1895
Questions to ask:
- Are the boys wearing special clothes while they exercise?
- Do you think these kinds of exercises might have been boring or fun?

Children playing musical games at Hartfield Crescent Elementary School, Birmingham *circa* 1930s
Question to ask:
- Do you ever play musical games to keep fit at your school?

Children attending gym classes at Danesfield County Primary School, Buckinghamshire, 1963
Question to ask:
- What do you wear for your PE lessons?

Taking a Break
Pages 16–17

Pupils eating their mid-day meal, school unknown, *circa* 1905
Question to ask:
- Do you think this was a good place to eat lunch?

Children eating school dinners, school unknown, *circa* 1950
Question to ask:
- Do you think the children are enjoying their school dinner?

Children drinking milk and playing 'shop', school unknown, *circa* 1960
Question to ask:
- Which healthy foods make a good snack at breaktime?

Having Fun at School
Pages 18–19

Hungerford School girls in their aprons who are celebrating the Hocktide Festival, *circa* 1910
Questions to ask:
- Do you think these girls look like they are wearing their best clothes?
- Do you think their teacher looks strict?

A boy and girl making Christmas cards in 1947
Question to ask:
- Have you ever tried printing? If you have, how did you do it?

Children at Newington Green Infants' School rehearsing for their Nativity Play, 1954
Questions to ask:
- Jesus and Mary are two characters in the play. Can you name any other characters on the stage?
- What are the children who are sitting below the stage doing?

Glossary

apparatus Equipment used for performing sports and PE, such as benches or mats.

chimney pots A pipe on top of a building out of which smoke from a fire can escape.

class register A book with the names of each pupil in a class which the teacher reads out every day to see who is present or absent from school.

deaf When somebody cannot hear anything.

drill The rules for doing something. These are usually practised over and over again.

Edwardian Describes something or someone from the time that King Edward VII ruled Britain (1901–1910).

equipment The tools, machines or things that you need for a particular purpose. A pair of scissors is the piece of equipment you need to cut paper.

government The people who make decisions about how a country is run.

healthy Describes something that is good for you, such as exercise. Can also be used to describe somebody who is fit and well.

level The height of a building. When a building has one floor, with no upper or lower levels, it is described as having one level.

lino Smooth shiny material which can be used to print. The design is cut out of the lino, then ink is rolled on top and the design can be printed onto a piece of paper.

logo A symbol or design that represents a particular school.

modern Describes something that is new or up-to-date.

museum A place where interesting objects are on display for people to see. Often these objects are old.

Nativity Play A play that tells the story of the birth of Jesus. Many schools perform the play at Christmas.

nature walk A walk on which children look and talk about plants, trees, flowers, animals, birds and insects.

object box A box filled with many objects used by teachers long ago during lessons.

overhead projector An electrical piece of equipment that a teacher uses to show pictures or words on a wall so the whole class can see.

pinafore A sleeveless kind of apron which covers a girl's dress.

private school A school where parents usually pay a fee for their child to attend.

rehearsing Practising something over and over again until you get it right.

rule Something that you must or must not do in a certain place. Being quiet when the teacher is talking to the class is a rule.

Second World War The war that broke out in 1939 and lasted until 1945.

school colours The colours that a particular school asks their children to wear. Trousers, skirts and jumpers should be worn in one colour such as navy blue or green.

separate/ separately Describes when something or some people are parted or divided.

strict/ stricter When somebody is strict they make you obey rules.

tape-recorders An electrical piece of equipment that is used to play or record music or voices.

Victorian Describes something or someone from the time that Queen Victoria ruled Britain (1837–1901)

Further Information

Books to Read
Non-fiction
History from Objects: At School
by Karen Bryant-Mole
(Hodder Wayland, 1996)
Home and School by Neil Morris
(Belitha Press, 2000)
School by Jane Shuter
(Heinemann, 1998)

Sources
Finding out About: Victorian Schools
by Amanda Clarke
(B. T. Batsford Limited, 1986)
Learning and Teaching in Victorian Times by P.F. Speed (Longman, 1983)

Websites
http://www.nettlesworth.durham.sch. uk/time/victorian/vschool.html
An interesting site where you can find out about Victorian schools. Discover more about lessons, classrooms, equipment and playtime.
http://www.kelsall.school.cheshire.org. uk/homeA.htm
Take a look at another modern school and compare it with your school. Kelsall School has all kinds of photographs of its school on this site, including pictures taken during lessons, photographs of its classrooms and dining room, and individual members of staff and pupils at work and play.

Places to Visit
The Museum of Childhood
Sudbury Hall, Sudbury DE6 5HT
Tel: 01283 585 305
Visit a reconstructed Victorian classroom.

The Ragged School Museum
46–50 Copperfield Road,
London E3 4RR
Tel: 020 8980 6405
Visit the school set up by Dr Barnardo over one hundred years ago.

Index